DATE DUE

DATE DUE

MAY 1 4 2008	
JUN 1 8 2008	
JUL 0 2 2008	
NOV 2 5 2008	
JUL 0 5 2012	

1398

DEMCO INC. 38-2931

POLAR MAMMALS

A TRUE BOOK

by

Larry Dane Brimner

Children's Press®
A Division of Grolier Publishing
New York London Hong Kong Sydney
Danbury, Connecticut

A harp seal

For my dear friend,
Nancy Adelle Hanssen

Reading Consultant
Linda Cornwell
Learning Resource Consultant
Indiana Department of
Education

Subject Consultant
Kathy Carlstead, Ph.D.
National Zoological Park
Smithsonian Institution

Library of Congress Cataloging-in-Publication Data

Brimner, Larry Dane.
    Polar mammals / by Larry Dane Brimner.
        p. cm. — (A true book)
    Summary: Describes such animals as the polar bear, ringed seal,
caribou, arctic hare, and wolverine and the ways they have adapted to
life in the frigid arctic regions.
    ISBN 0-516-20042-9 (lib.bdg.)   ISBN 0-516-26112-6 (pbk.)
    1. Mammals—Arctic regions—Juvenile literature. [1. Mammals.—
Arctic regions.] I. Title. II. Series.
QL736.B69   1996
599.0998—dc20
                          96-34192
                              CIP
                              AC

Contents

The Arctic is a wilderness covered with snow and ice during the winter (above); spring and summer are short, and animals must use the time to prepare for winter.

A Difficult World

Month after month, snow and ice cover the ground in the northern wilderness called the Arctic. Biting winds howl across the landscape. For several weeks in winter, the sun never rises above the horizon. It is a vast, frigid, and difficult world.

With the arrival of spring and then summer, large areas of ice begin to melt. In some places, there are endless hours of daylight. Even so, life is difficult for arctic animals. The ground never truly thaws. And the spring and summer seasons are very short. Only unique animals can live in such a harsh environment.

How have animals special-ized or adapted for life in the Arctic? One feature of arctic

A layer of blubber protects beluga whales from the cold Arctic waters.

animals is warm blood. Cold-blooded animals—such as frogs, snakes, and lizards—do not live here. They would freeze to death because their body temperature becomes the same as the air surrounding them. Warm-blooded animals are able to maintain an almost constant body temperature no matter how cold or warm the air gets.

A thick layer of hair protects many Arctic animals. During the summer, musk oxen lose their winter coats.

Some arctic animals also have a layer of fat or blubber just beneath the skin. The fat is like a blanket. It helps the animal stay warm.

Other animals have two layers of hair. A soft, woolly inner layer—called ground hair or underfur—keeps the animal warm. An outer layer—called guard hairs—protects the ground hair from dampness.

Even the hair itself may be specialized. Sometimes it is

hollow. Hollow hairs help in two ways. The air inside the hairs protects the animals against the cold. It also helps them stay afloat in water. A polar bear's hairs are both hollow and transparent. Its fur works like a portable greenhouse. Whatever sunlight is available passes through the hair. It warms the polar bear's black skin. The warmth is trapped inside the fur.

Unique "greenhouse" hair helps to protect polar bears (above). No matter how wet they get on the outside, sea otters and seals stay dry under their thick hair (right).

Sometimes the hair is extra thick. Sea otters and seals have hair so thick the Arctic's frigid water never touches their skin.

Polar Bears and Seals

A polar bear lies quietly on the ice. It looks as if it is resting, but it isn't. With its sharp sense of smell, it has found a hole in the ice. It is waiting for a seal. Seals are a polar bear's favorite food, and polar bears can be very

A polar bear (above) waits at a seal hole; a polar bear's paw (left) is large and strong. A single blow with it can be deadly.

Ringed seals are year-round Arctic residents.

patient. The polar bear will wait for hours if necessary.

Ringed seals live in the Arctic year-round. They are well designed for life in this difficult world. Half their body weight is made up of blubber! In warm weather, blood flows

Ringed seals are most vulnerable when they are on land.

into their flippers and is cooled. But when the temperature is icy cold, very little blood flows into the flippers. Their flippers are a unique heating and cooling system!

Like other marine mammals, ringed seals cannot breathe

A harp seal surfaces at its breathing hole. Like ringed seals, they must surface for air about every eight minutes.

underwater. But they need oxygen to survive. They use their sharp teeth and flippers to cut breathing holes in the ice. They must come to the surface to breathe about every eight minutes. They visit the holes regularly to make sure they remain free of ice.

Today, luck is with the polar bear and not the seal. When the seal surfaces for air, the polar bear strikes out with its powerful paw. The seal is flipped onto the ice and killed instantly. The polar bear has caught a nice seal meal.

Arctic Foxes and Lemmings

As soon as the polar bear wanders away, an arctic fox approaches what is left of the seal. Polar bears usually eat only the blubber of a seal. Arctic foxes often follow polar bears and wait patiently too—for leftovers.

Arctic foxes live year-round

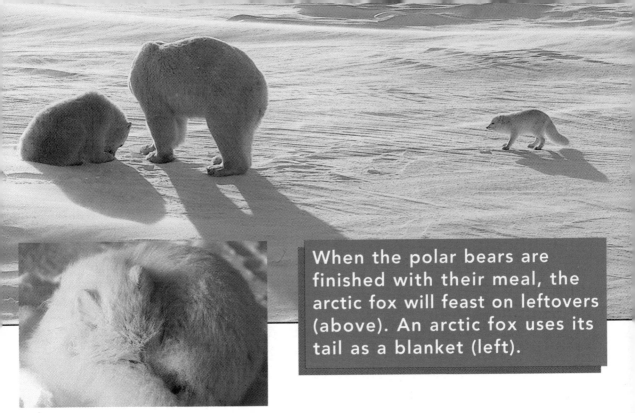

When the polar bears are finished with their meal, the arctic fox will feast on leftovers (above). An arctic fox uses its tail as a blanket (left).

in the North. Like polar bears and arctic hares, arctic foxes have hair on the bottoms of their feet. The hair helps to keep their feet warm. It also makes travel on ice and snow easier.

During the summer, the arctic fox changes color (above). White fur is good camouflage during the winter (right).

Changing color to match their surroundings is another way some animals are specialized to survive life in the Arctic. Many animals in this part of the world turn pure white in the winter. One kind of arctic fox camouflages itself this way. The other kind of arctic fox remains blue-gray throughout the year. There is less snow where it lives, so it doesn't need camouflage as much.

When they are not eating leftovers or raiding birds' nests, arctic foxes usually

This arctic fox has captured a lemming for a meal.

A collared lemming peers out from its tunnel.

hunt for lemmings. Lemmings are small mouselike rodents about the size of guinea pigs. They also live year-round in the Arctic. They are the main food of arctic foxes. Many other arctic animals prey on them too.

Like other lemmings, collared lemmings are vegetarians. They feed on plants, berries, and roots. They are the only lemmings who turn pure white in winter. Long hair on their legs helps them stay warm. Hair on the soles of their feet gives them traction in their icy tunnels under the snow.

Lemmings are known for their unusual behavior. About every four years, their winter tunnels and burrows become overcrowded. There is not enough food for all the lemmings. When spring arrives and the snow begins to melt, the lemmings try to move to less crowded areas. This is called migration. They begin by making a mad dash in one direction. Nothing can stop them. They run over rocks. They swim through streams and try to swim across the ocean. For their predators, it is a time of feasting. Most

of the lemmings that do not drown or get eaten make their way into the forests.

Nature provides a balance, though. Following a "lemming year," other animals cannot find enough food either. Many starve to death. Others become prey.

Besides warmth, arctic hares cluster for protection (above). Wolverines are the largest members of the weasel family (left).

Arctic Hares and Wolverines

Some distance from the arctic fox, a group of arctic hares gathers on the tundra, or prairie. It is treeless here, but there is vegetation for the hares to eat. They cluster together for warmth. Sometimes as many as 120 hares form a huddle. Most rabbits have large ears. Arctic hares have very small ears. This helps them to conserve their body heat. Their large hind feet act like snowshoes. They have no trouble bounding over snow when it's winter.

An enemy silently approaches. It is a wolverine, the largest member of the weasel family. It charges suddenly into the cluster of hares. But the group provides protection as well as warmth. All at once, the hares scatter

A wolverine (left) on the hunt; when attacked the hares (below) scatter for cover.

in different directions. They take shelter behind rocks and inside cracks. This wild activity seems to confuse the wolverine. It doesn't know which way to run. So it gives up. For now, it settles for some wild berries.

Caribou move along the same migration trails season after season (above). The broad antler that grows forward is called a shovel (right). Caribou must move with their heads held back so that their antlers don't throw them off balance (below).

Caribou

In another part of the tundra, barren-ground caribou move along a trail. They use trails that have been carved for thousands of years by their ancestors. They are noisy travelers, grunting and coughing as they make their way. They hold their heads back stiffly as they move. In this way their massive antlers don't throw them off balance. Caribou are the only members of the deer family in which both males and females have antlers. Each has one broad antler, called a shovel, which grows forward. Caribou use it to dig through snow for hidden vegetation.

Caribou migrate northward in the spring. There, cows give birth to their young in the high, rocky hills. Summer and early

Season after season, caribou forage on grasses, mosses, and lichens (right). Moose like the tender, new grasses that grow in tundra lakes, ponds, and streams (left).

fall are spent on the tundra. Here, they can graze on grasses, mosses, and lichens. In late autumn, they will return to the forests bordering the tundra. This is where they will spend the winter.

Moose

At a tundra lake, a moose wades into the water. Moose are the largest members of the deer family. They are bigger than caribou. The webbing of their antlers is also more obvious. The moose feed on new grasses growing in the lake and many other kinds of vegetation.

Moose are the
largest members
of the deer family.
The webbing of a
moose's antlers
gives them a
solid, heavy look.

Long hair helps protect the musk oxen from the weather and from mosquitoes!

Musk oxen and Arctic Wolves

A herd of musk oxen is grazing on the short tundra grasses. They do not like to share their territory with other animals. For this reason, they remain apart.

Musk oxen look bigger than they really are. They are mostly hair. At a musk oxen's neck, chest, and rump, the hair may be 2 to 3 feet (0.6 to 1.0 meters) long! The hair protects them from the cold of winter. It also protects them from the many mosquitoes of the tundra summer.

A pack of arctic wolves spy the herd of musk oxen. Wolves work together to capture their prey. Sometimes they hunt small animals, like hares and lemmings. But they usually attack caribou, moose,

Arctic wolves sometimes work together to trap their prey. These arctic wolves have killed a caribou (above). An arctic wolf (right).

and musk oxen. They prey on sick, weak, or young animals, because these animals sometimes fall behind the rest of the herd. They are easy targets for wolves.

Musk oxen form a circle to fend off their foes.

The musk oxen sense danger. The adults form a tight circle around the younger animals. They charge out at the attacking wolves. They try to gore the wolves with their horns. Today, luck is with the musk oxen. The wolves retreat and will hunt for a meal somewhere else.

Winter or summer, the Arctic is a difficult world. To survive, animals depend on their own special features. They also depend on one another. The failure of even one species threatens the survival of all the others. There is much for humans to learn from the Arctic's delicate balance.

Did you know this?

Polar bears sometimes swim far into the ocean. They have been seen more than a hundred miles from the nearest land.

An arctic fox's eyes look more like a cat's than a dog's. The oval pupil opens wide to help the fox see better at night and it closes to a sliver so that the fox can see in bright light.

Eyes of arctic fox

Polar bear swimming

Musk ox close-up

musk oxen get their name from a musk gland under each eye. When attacked, they rub the gland on their legs and release an unpleasant odor. This discourages an enemy from getting too close.

Arctic hares are North America's largest hares.

Arctic hare

To Find Out More

Here are some additional resources to help you learn more about mammals of the polar regions:

 **Books**

 **Organizations**

Brandenburg, Jim. **To the Top of the World: Adventures with Arctic Wolves.** Walker and Company, 1993.

Matthews, Downs. **Arctic Foxes.** Simon & Schuster, 1995.

Miller, Debbie S. **A Caribou Journey.** Little, Brown & Company, 1994.

Pandell, Karen. **Land of Dark, Land of Light.** The Arctic National Wildlife Refuge, 1993.

Arctic National Wildlife Refuge
101 12th Avenue, Box 20
Fairbanks, AK 99701
E-mail: *R7ANWR@mail. fws.gov*

Canadian Wildlife Service
Environment Canada
Ottawa, Ontario
K1A 0H3
Telephone: (819) 997-1095

International Wolf Center
1396 Highway 169
Ely, Minnesota 55731-8129
Telephone: (800) ELY-WOLF
E-mail: *wolfinfo@wolf.org*

Sea World of California
Education Department
1720 South Shores Road
San Diego, CA 92109-7995
(619) 226-3834

**U.S. Fish and
Wildlife Service**
Region 7 Office
1011 E. Tudor Road
Anchorage, AK 99503
Telephone: (907) 786-3486
Fax: (907) 786-3306
E-mail: *R7PA@mail.fws.gov*

The Yukon Trail. MECC.
Journey over snow-
covered mountains,
watch a dogsled race,
learn about arctic wildlife,
and more. Ages 7+

Zurk's Alaskan Trek.
Soleil's Whole World.
Learning Series
Explore the northern
ecosystems, learn about
animals, create stories,
and improve your math—
all at the same time!
Ages 6-10

Electronic Zoo
Visit the zoo without
leaving home!
*http://www.zi.biologie.
unimuenchen.de/~st2042/
exotic.html*

The Mickey Moose Club
Membership information,
moose calendars,
pictures, and more
great moose stuff.
*http://www.halcyon.com/
moose/welcome.html*

Musk Oxen
Find out more about these
fascinating animals.
*http://bluegoose.arw.rq.
fws.gov/NWRSFiles/Refuge
SystemLeaflets/R7/Arctic/
FactSheets/FactSheetMusk
Oxen.html*

45

Important Words

camouflage to hide or conceal by blending in with one's surroundings

ground hair the soft, woolly inner layer of fur that keeps arctic animals warm

guard hairs the outer layer of fur that protects the ground hair from dampness

migration to move from one region to another

shovel the broad antler used by caribou to dig through soil and snow

tundra the level plain of the Arctic that consists of a black, mucky soil and a permanently frozen subsoil

Index

Meet the Author

Larry Dane Brimner, a native of Florida, grew up in Alaska and California. A teacher for twenty years, he is now the author of more than thirty fiction and nonfiction books for young people. When he isn't writing, he visits elementary schools throughout the country to discuss the writing process with young authors and readers. He relaxes by gardening, reading a good mystery, or taking a spin on his mountain bike in Colorado's San Juan Mountains.